JLo
VIDEO VANGUARD
RECIPEIENT

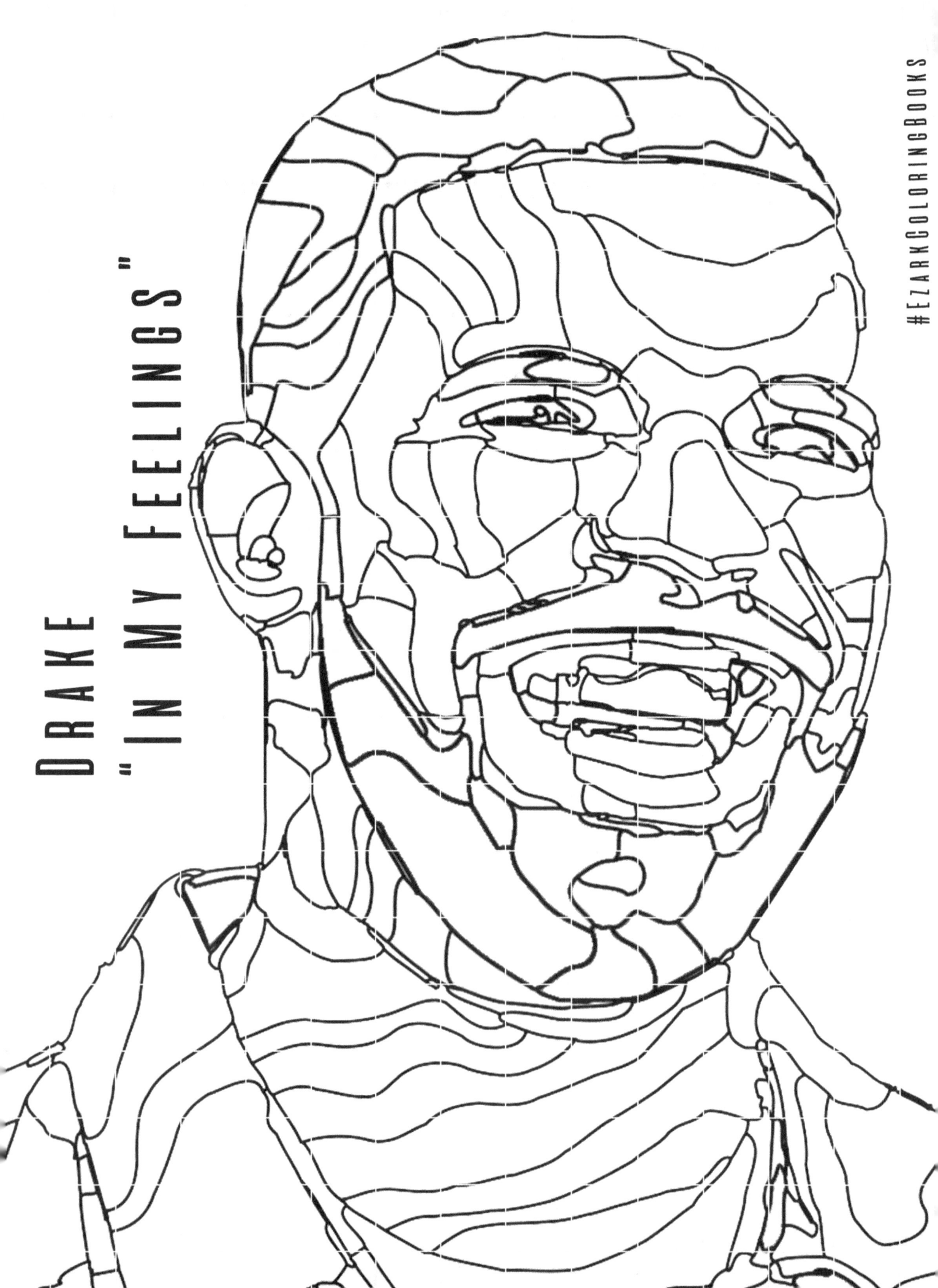

DRAKE
"IN MY FEELINGS"

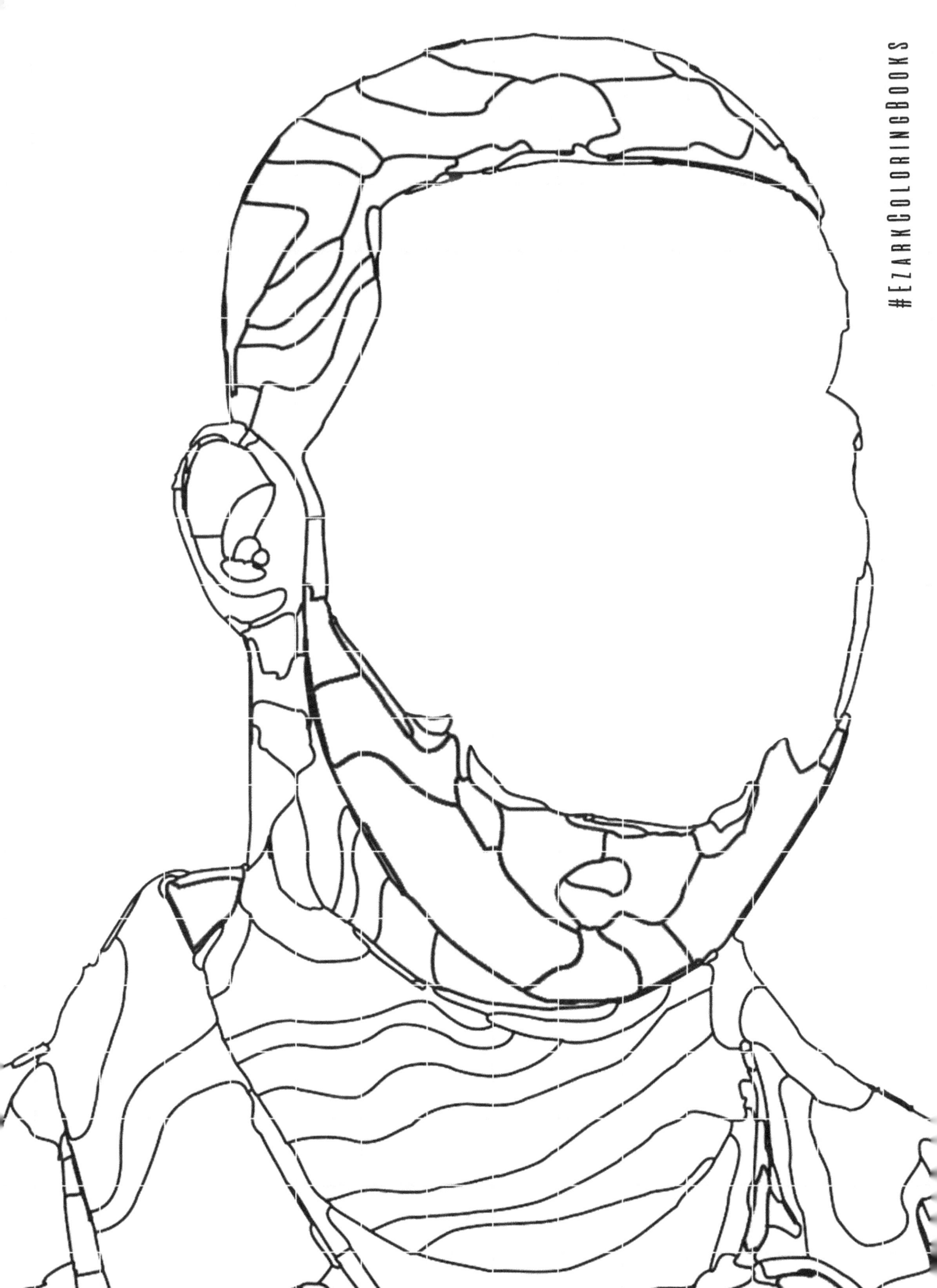

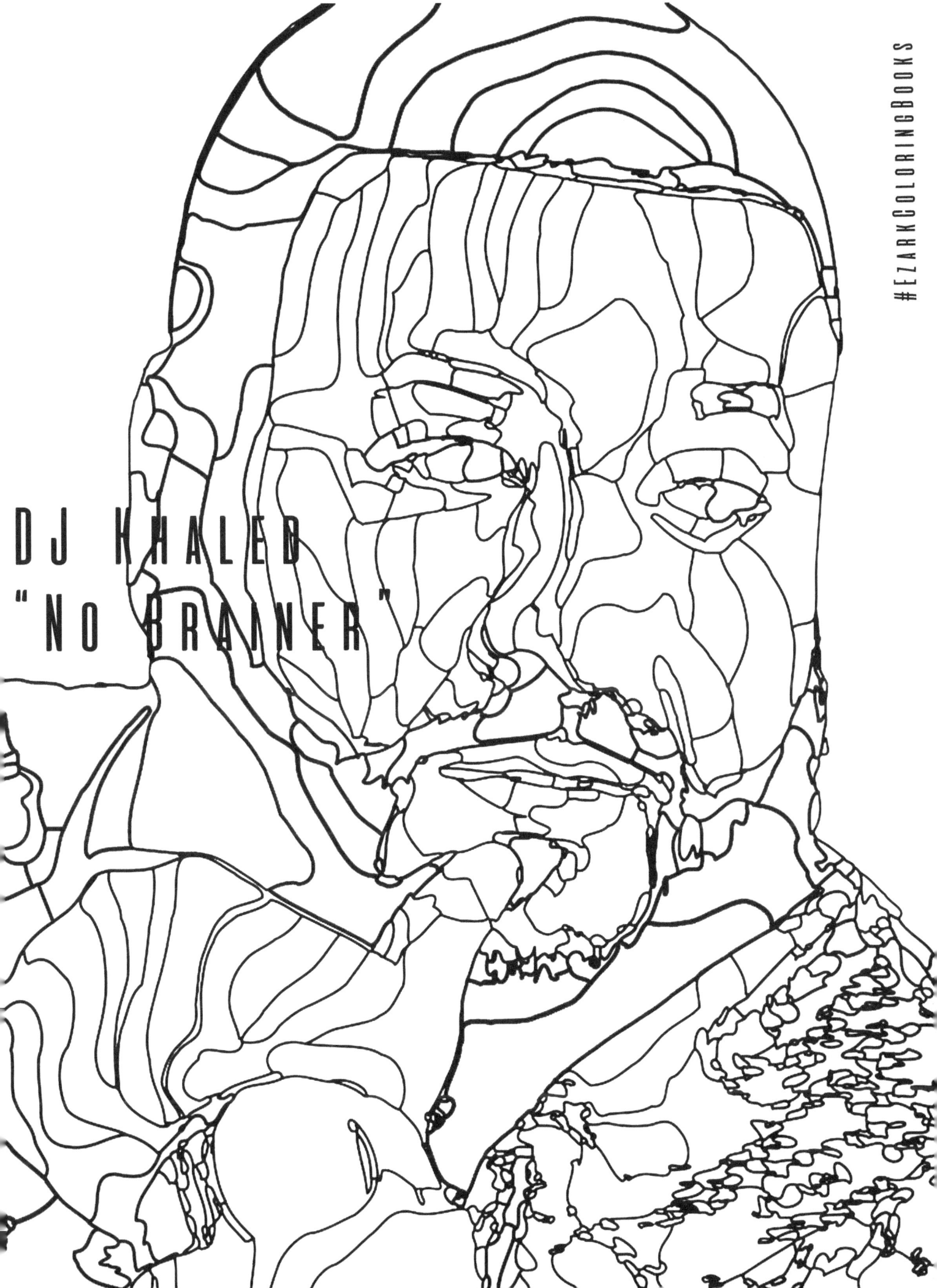

DJ KHALED
"NO BRAINER"

JUSTIN BIEBER
"NO BRAINER"

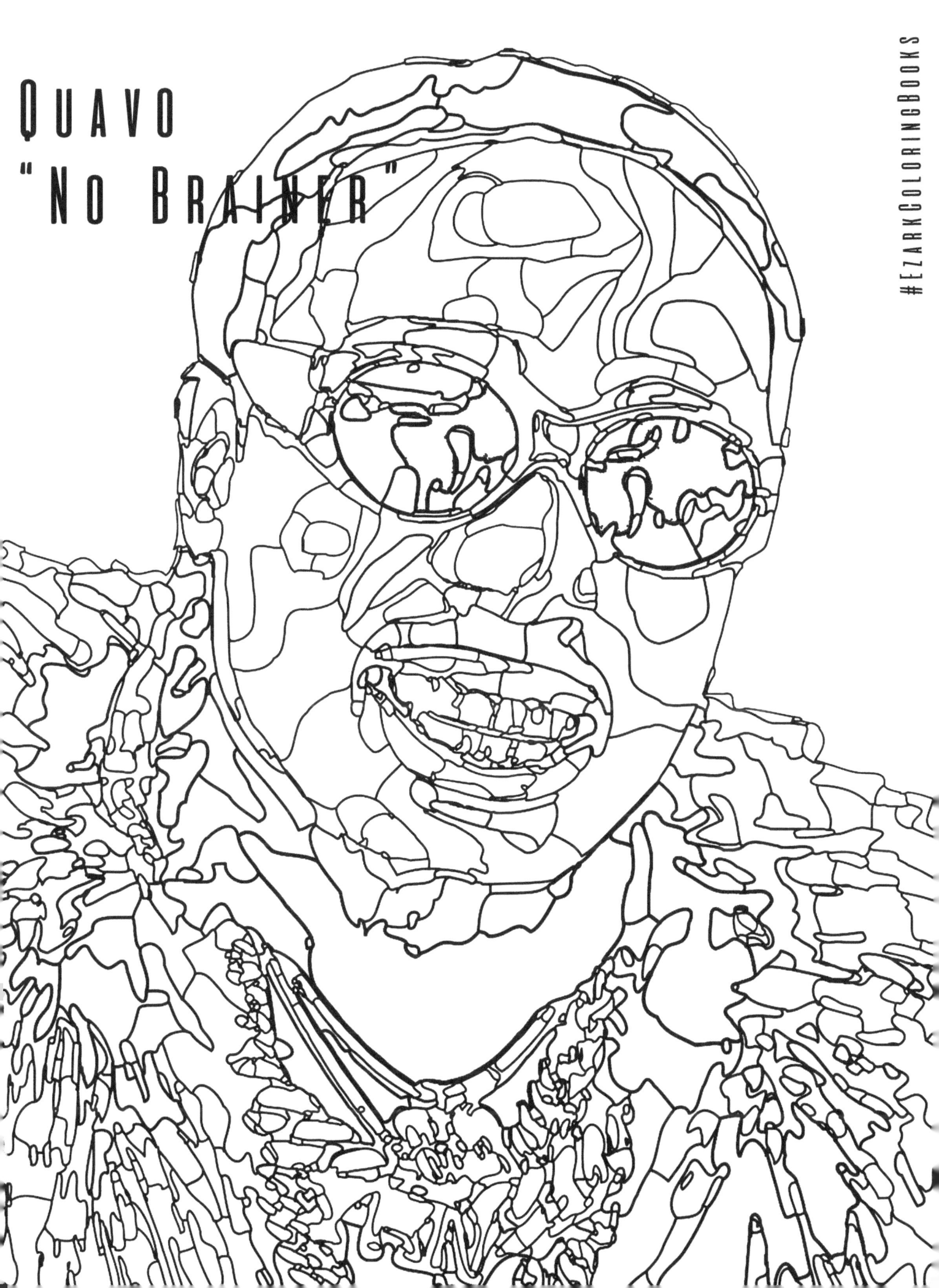

CHANCE THE RAPPER
"NO BRAINER"

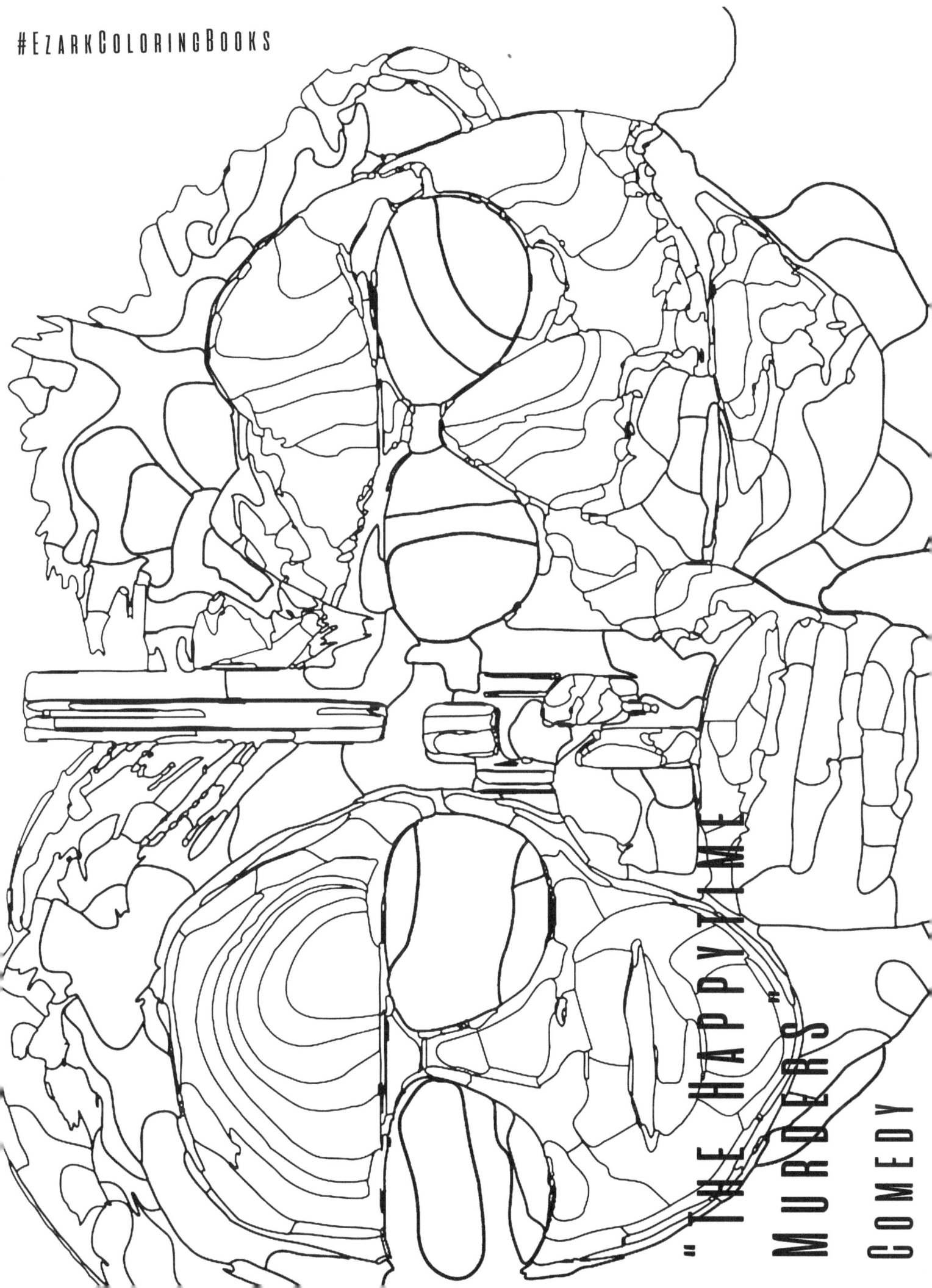

"The Happytime Murders"

Comedy

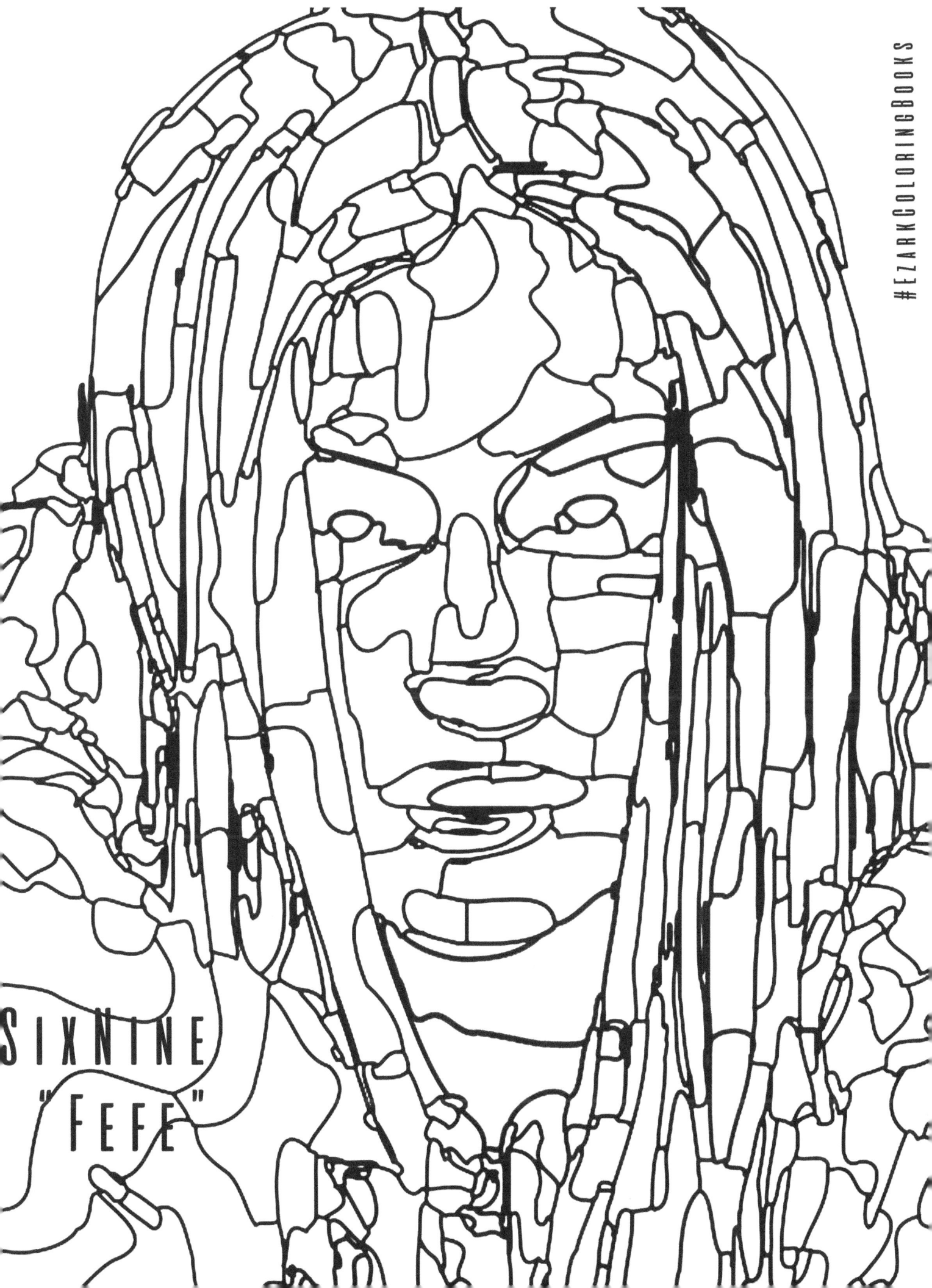

SIXNINE
"FEFE"

Bebe Rexha
"Meant To Be"

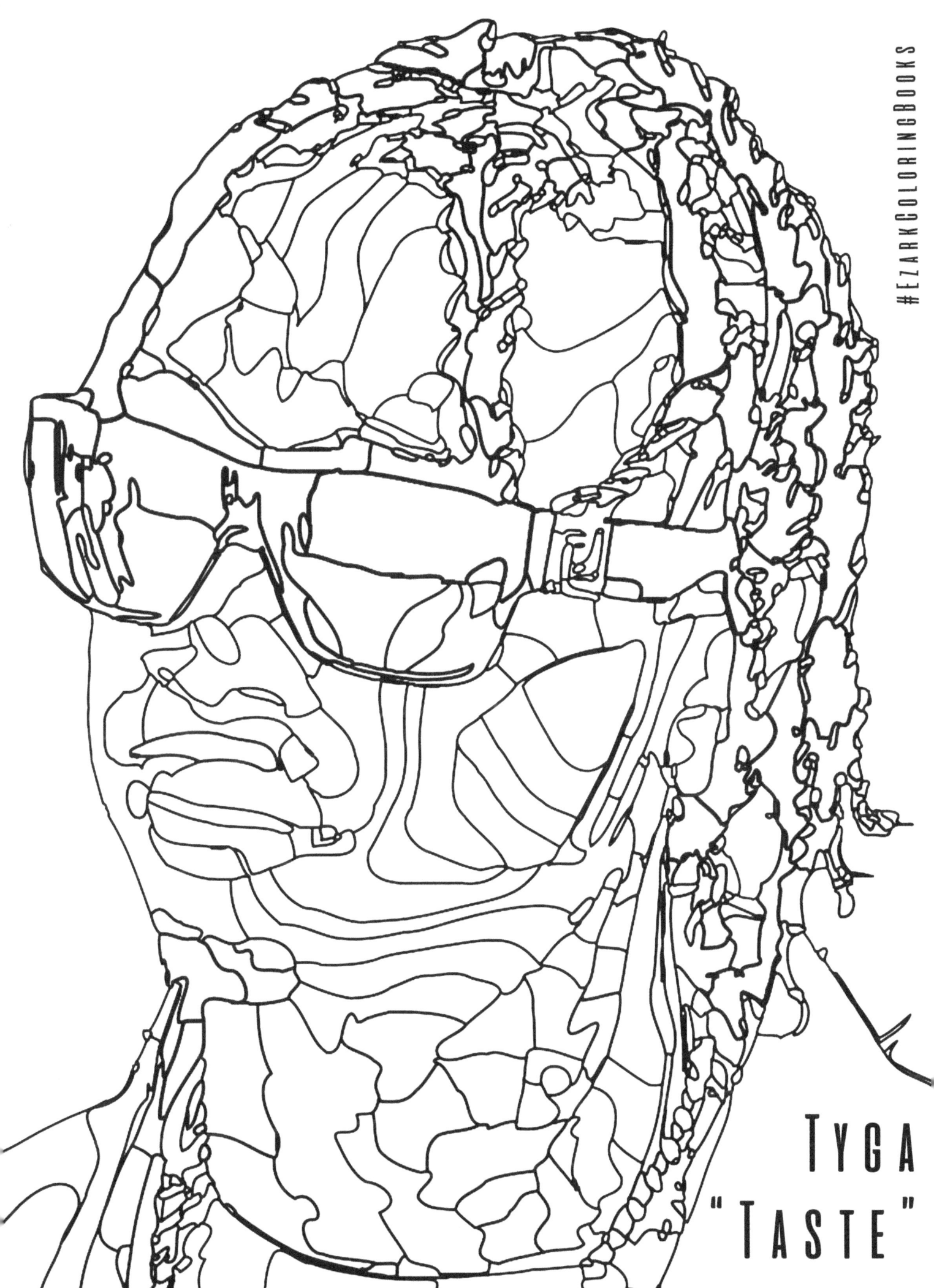

#EZARKCOLORINGBOOKS

Tyga
"Taste"

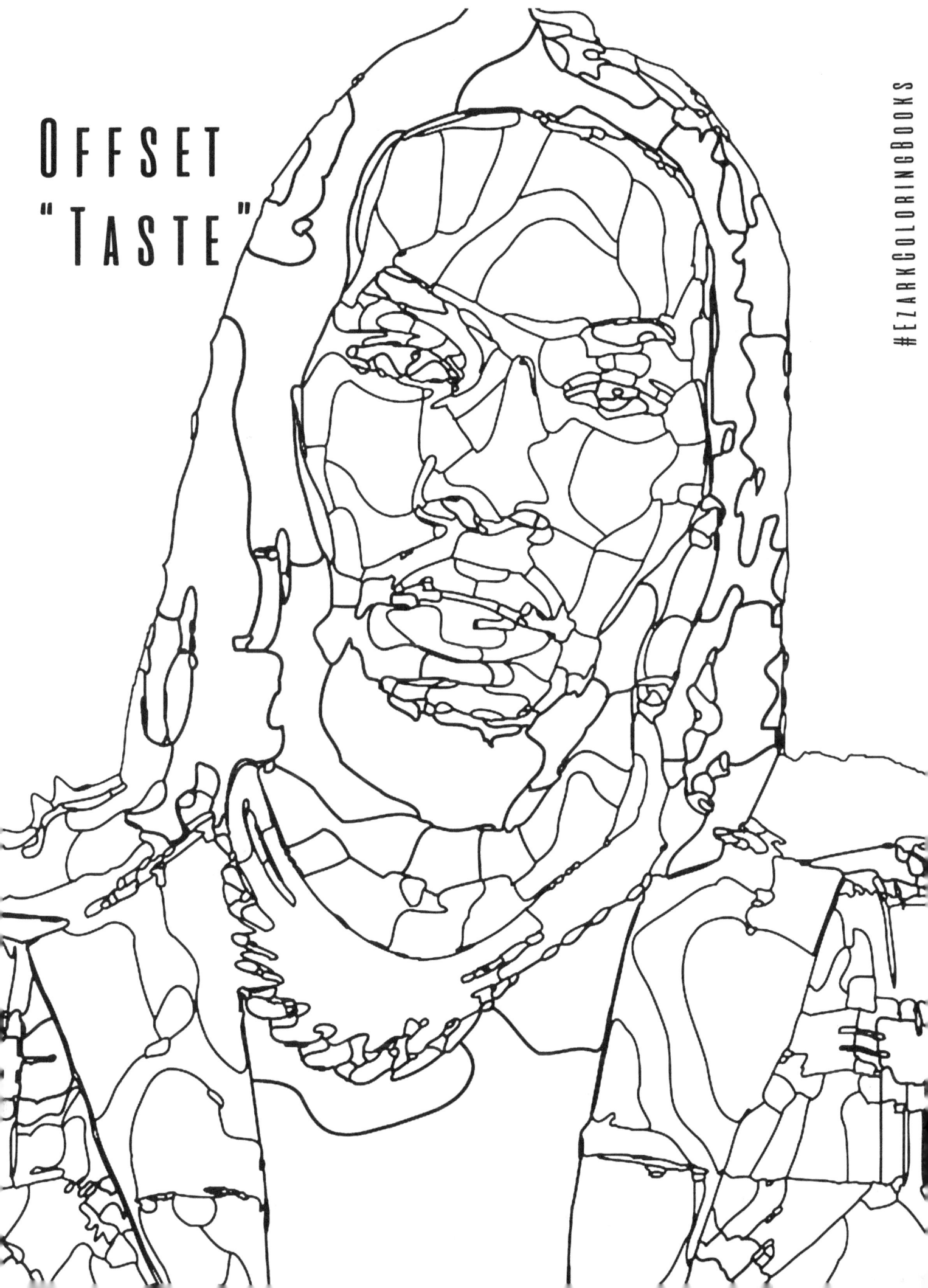

Offset
"Taste"

KHALID
"LOVE LIES"

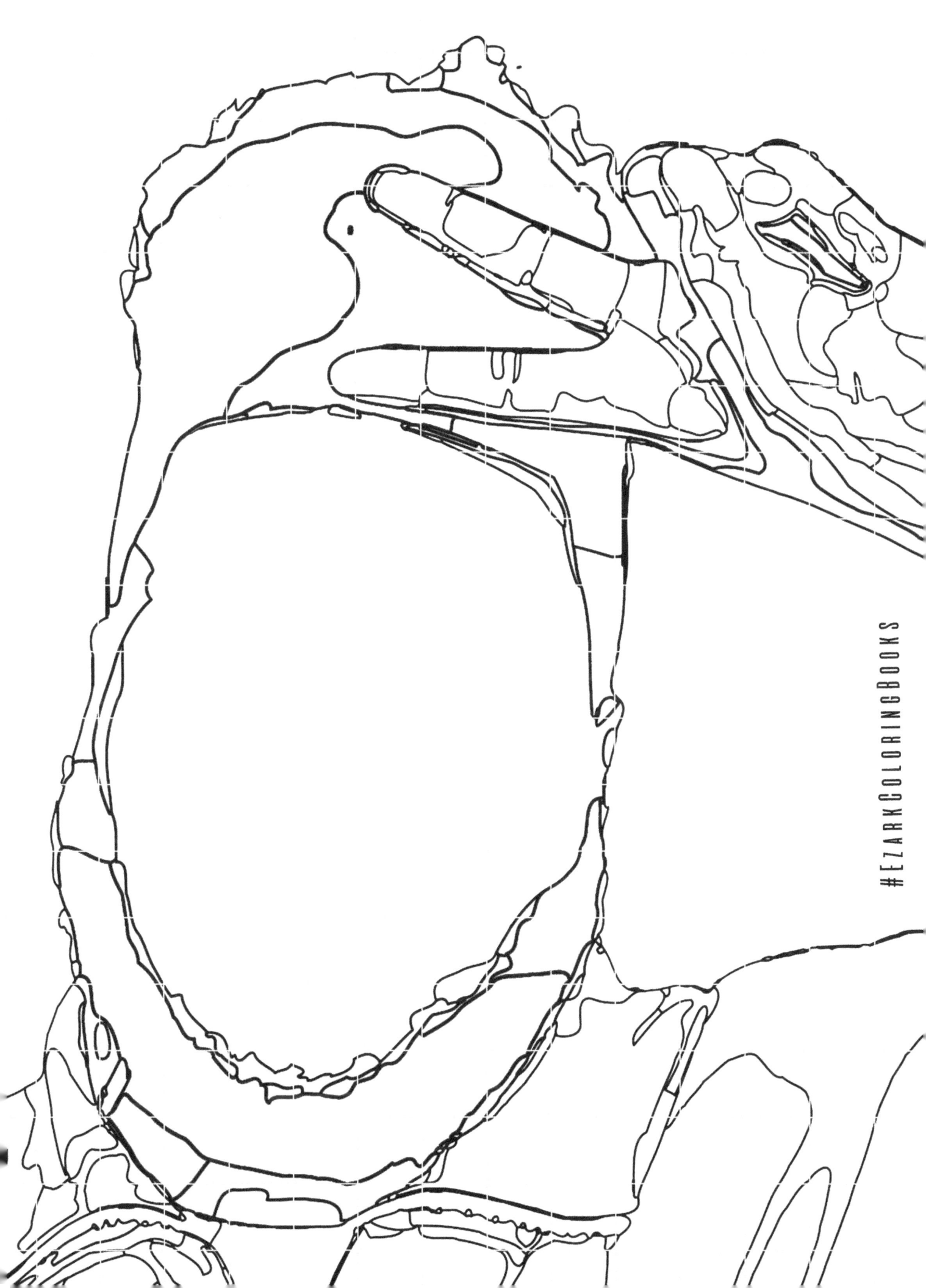

NORMANI
"LOVE LIES"

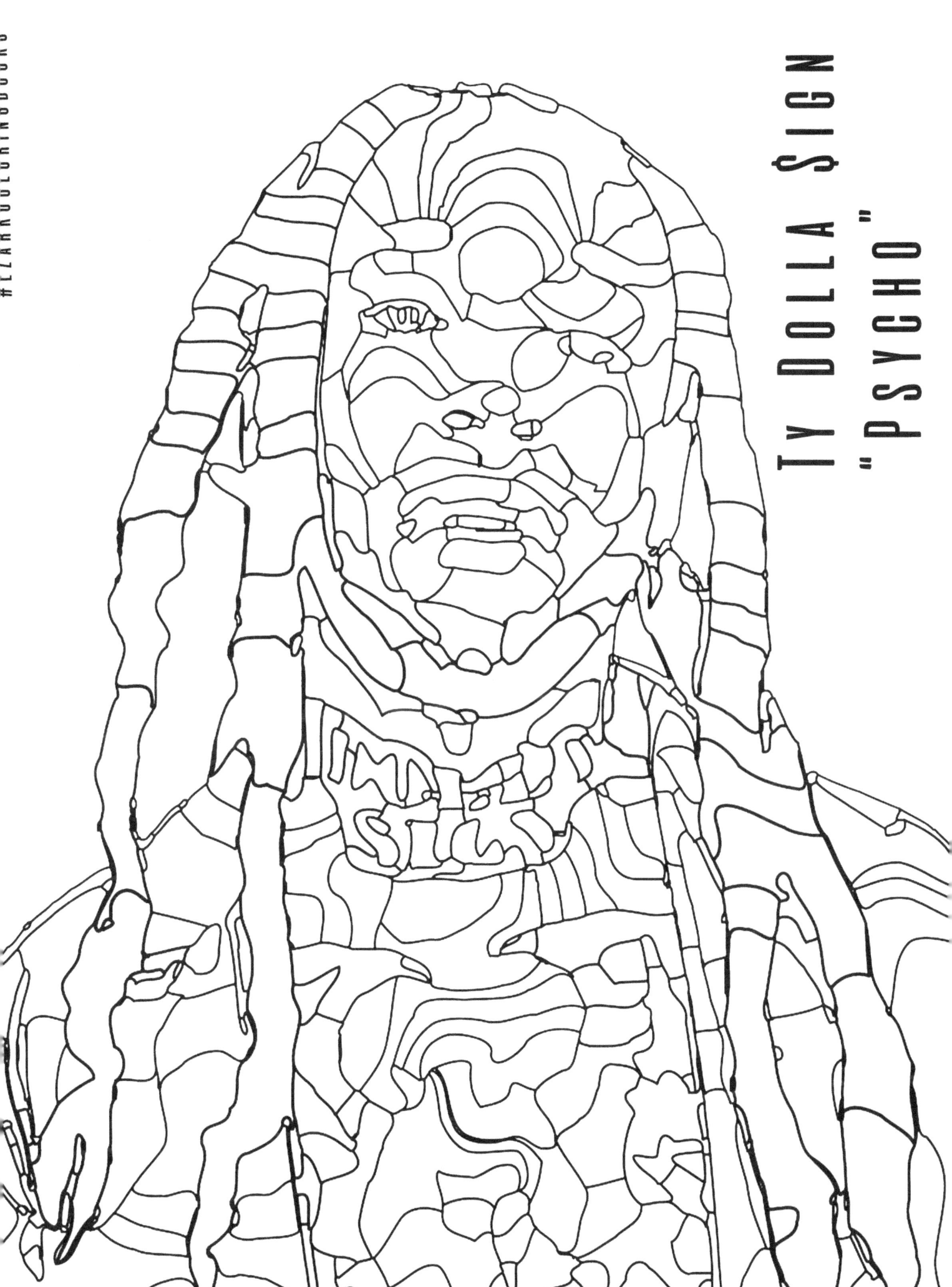

TY DOLLA $IGN
"PSYCHO"

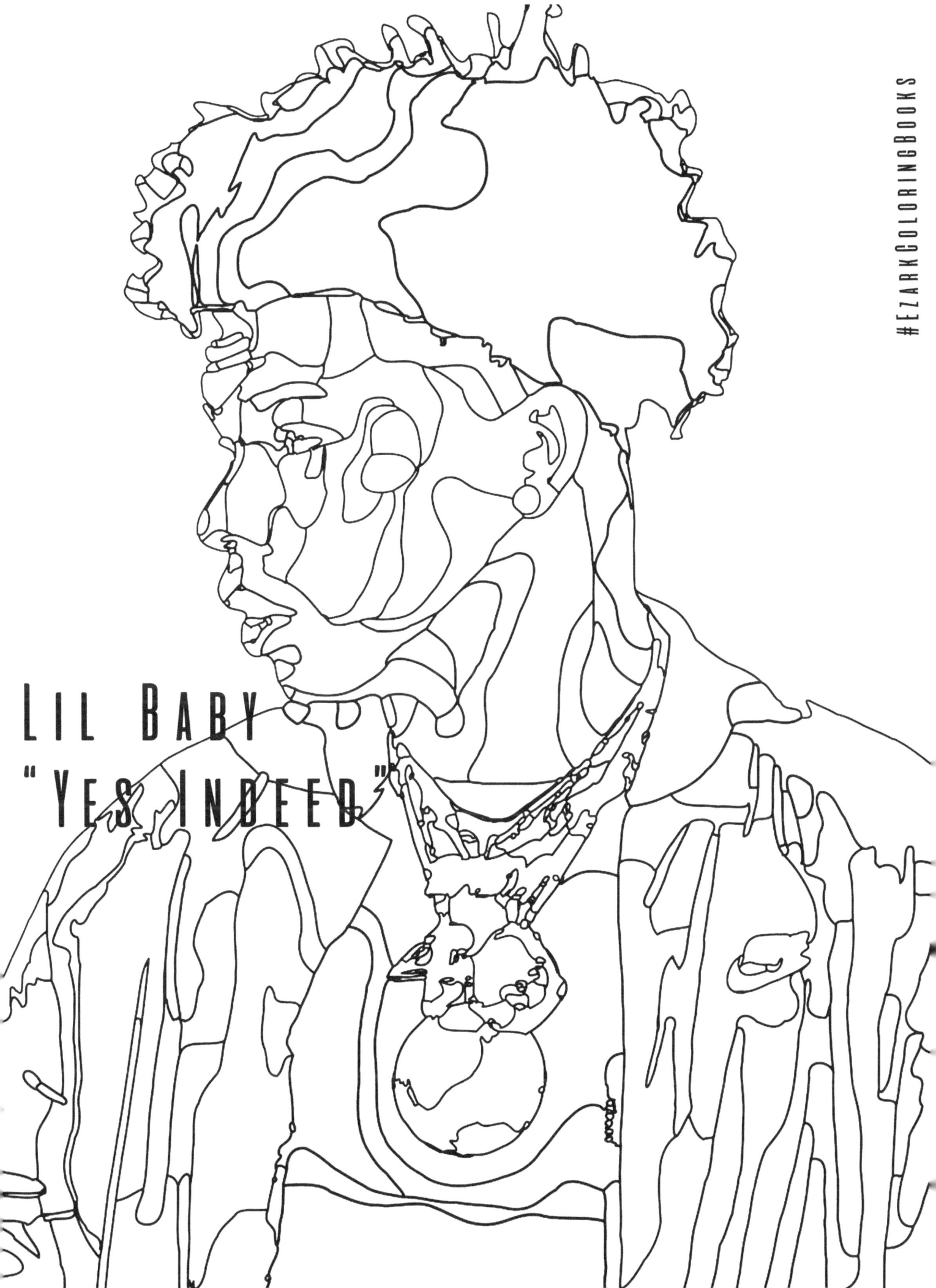

Lil Baby
"Yes Indeed"

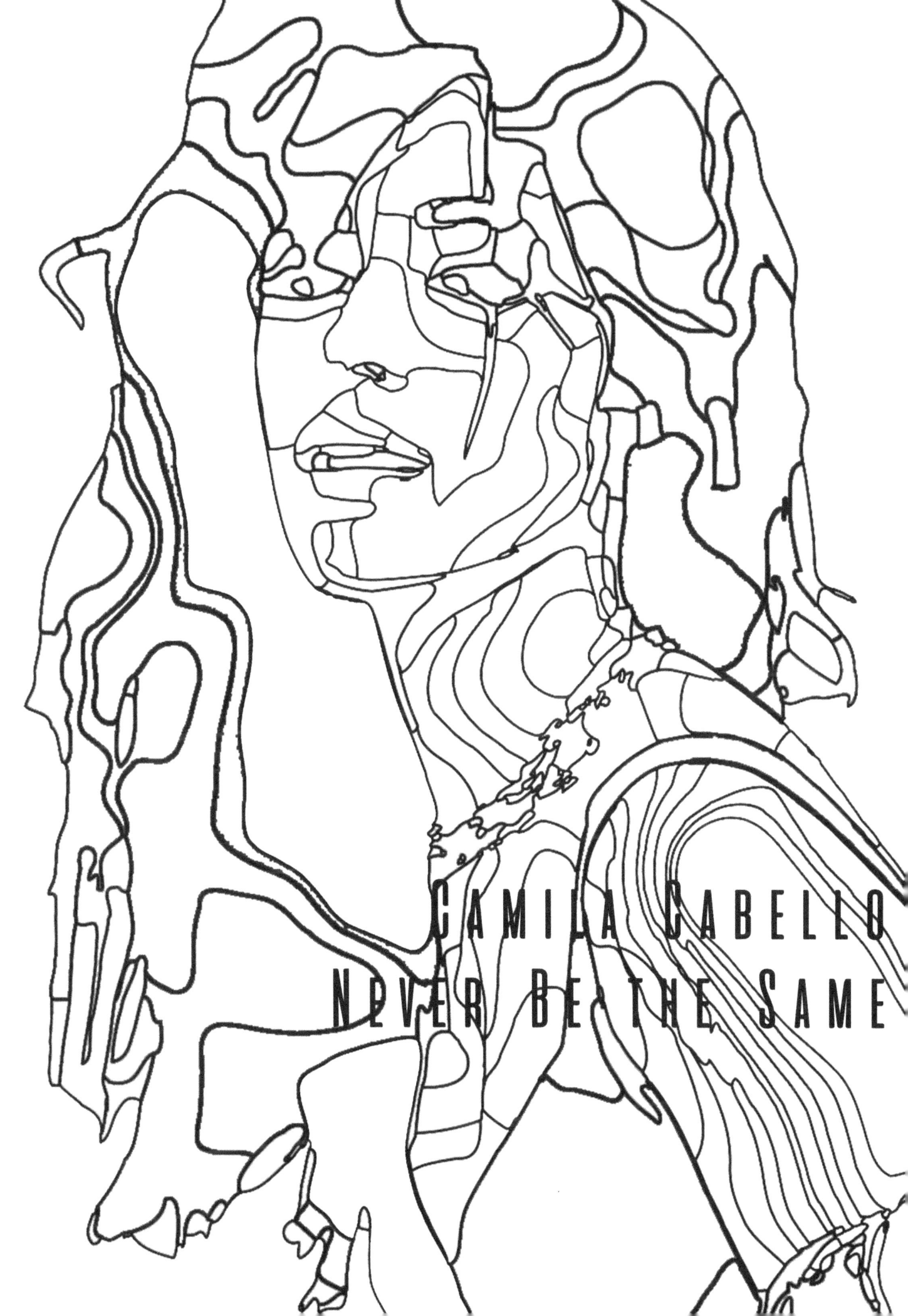

Camila Cabello

Never Be the Same

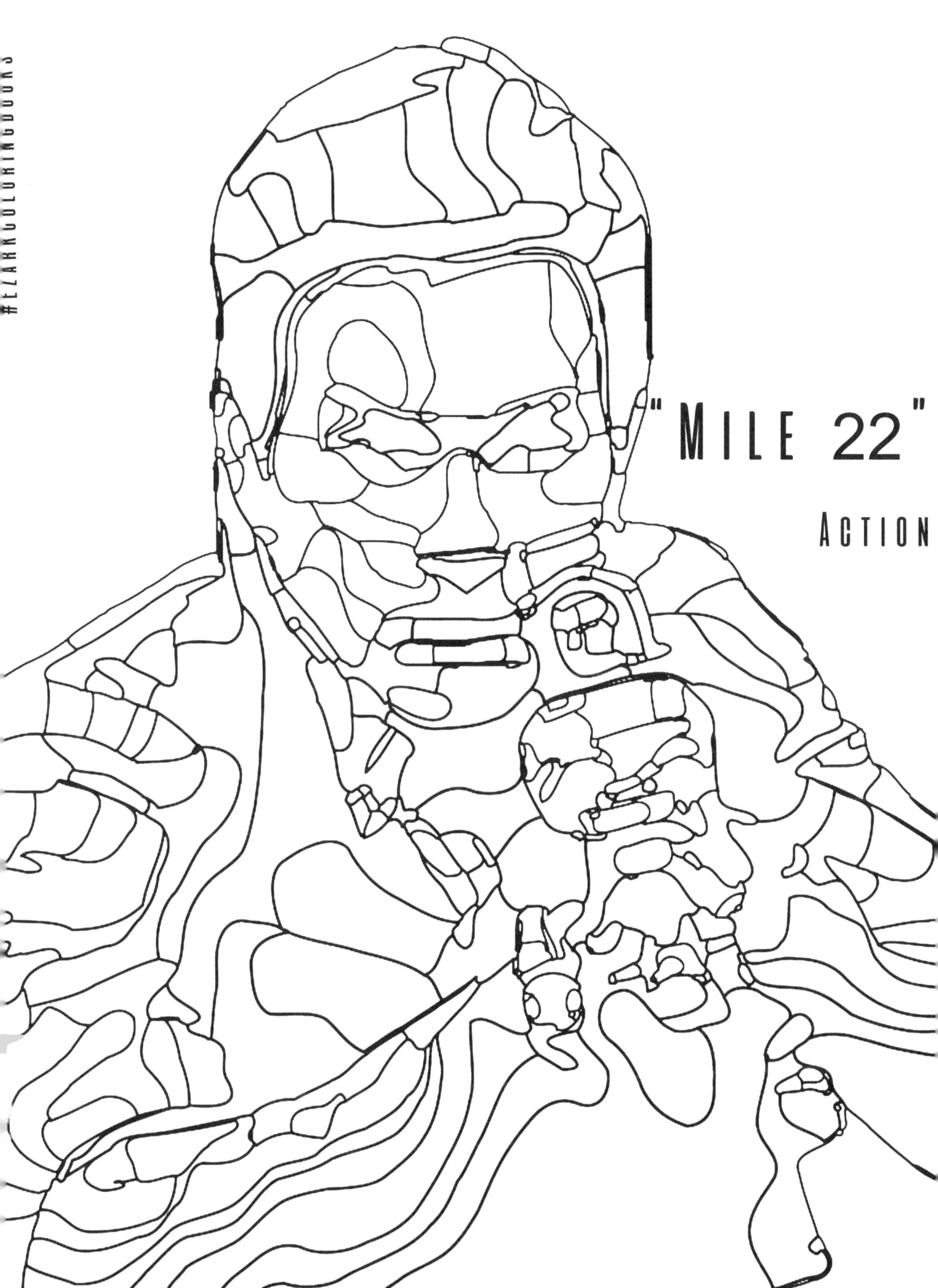

"MILE 22"

ACTION

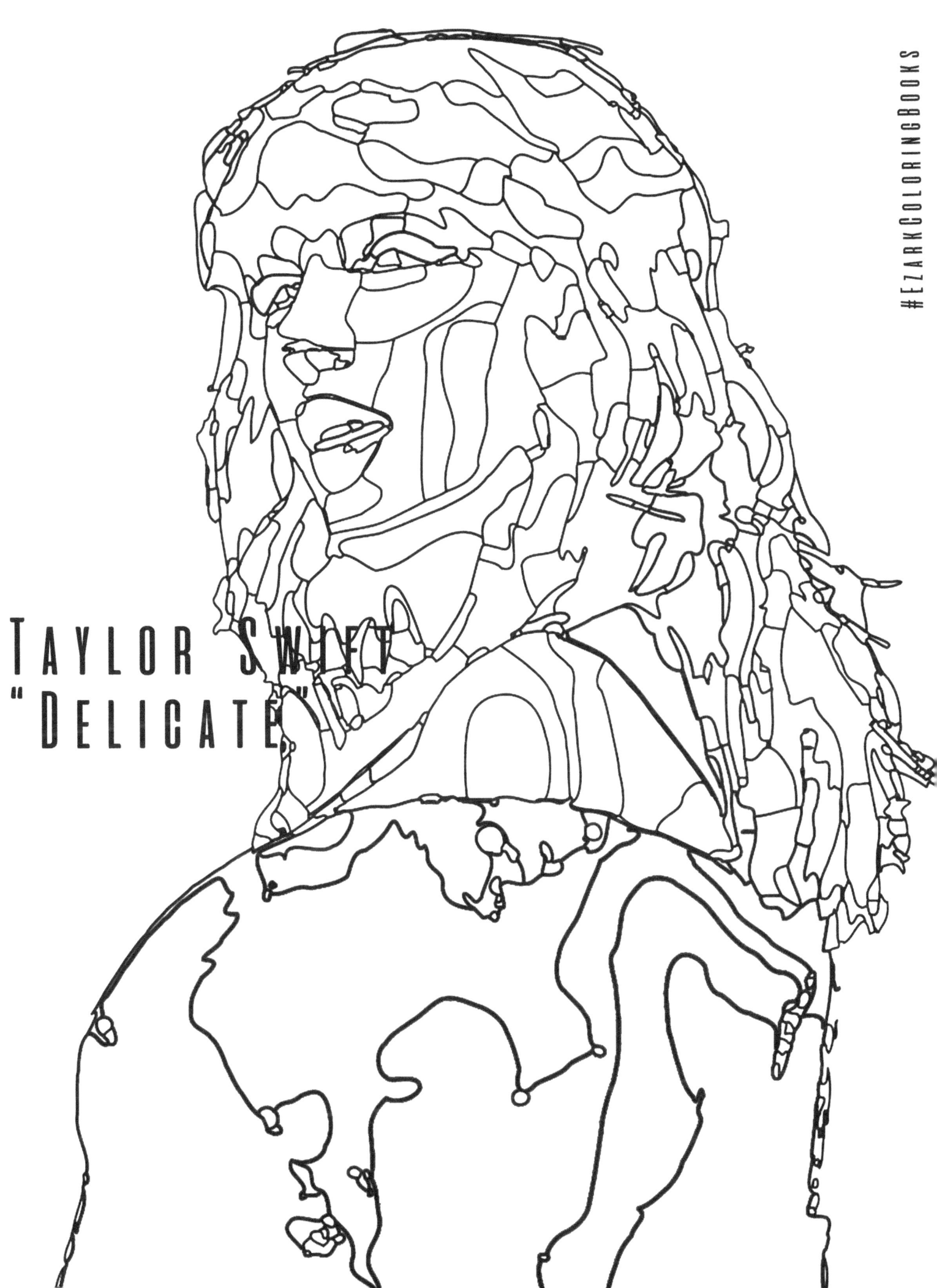

Taylor Swift
"Delicate"

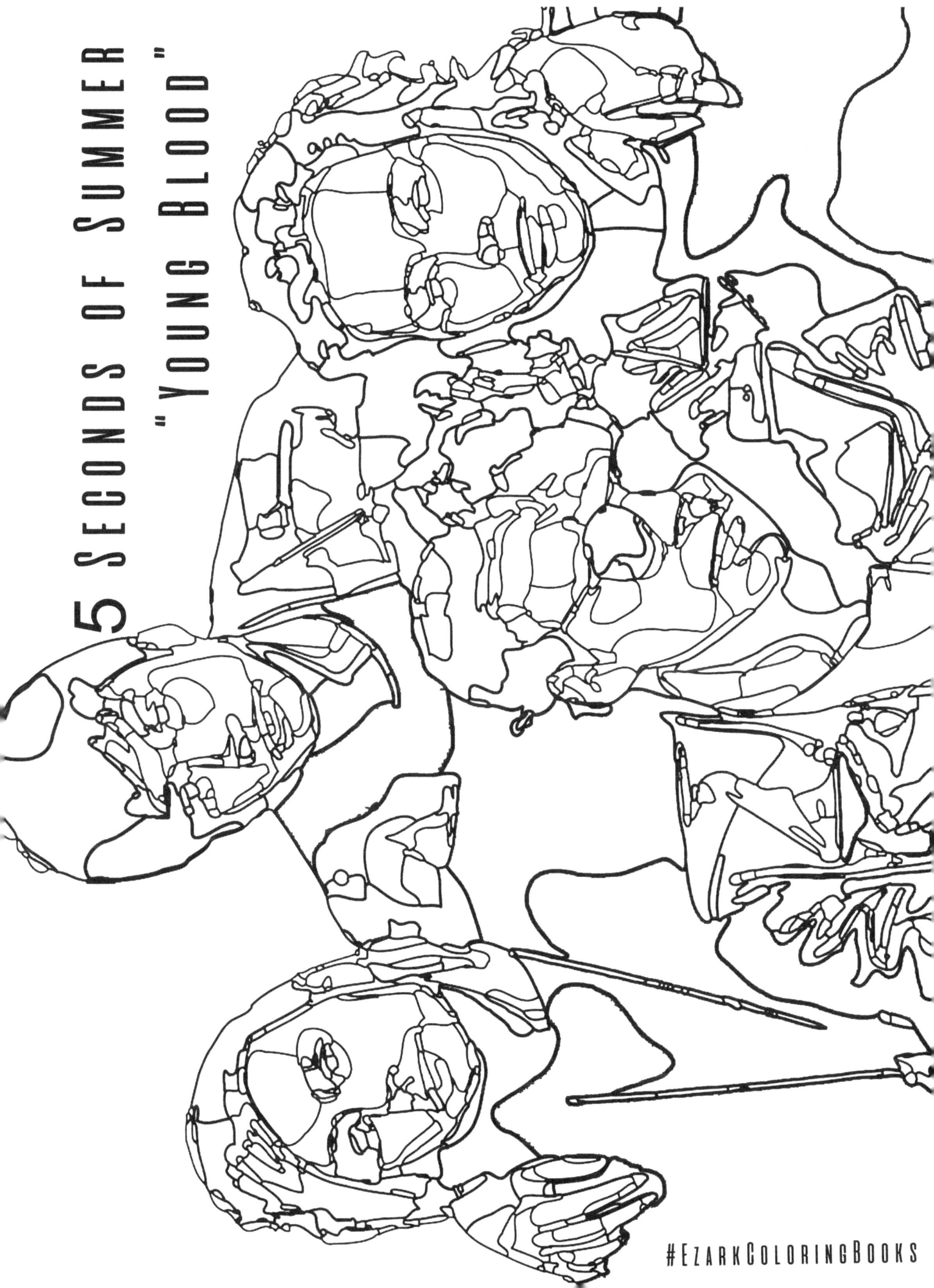

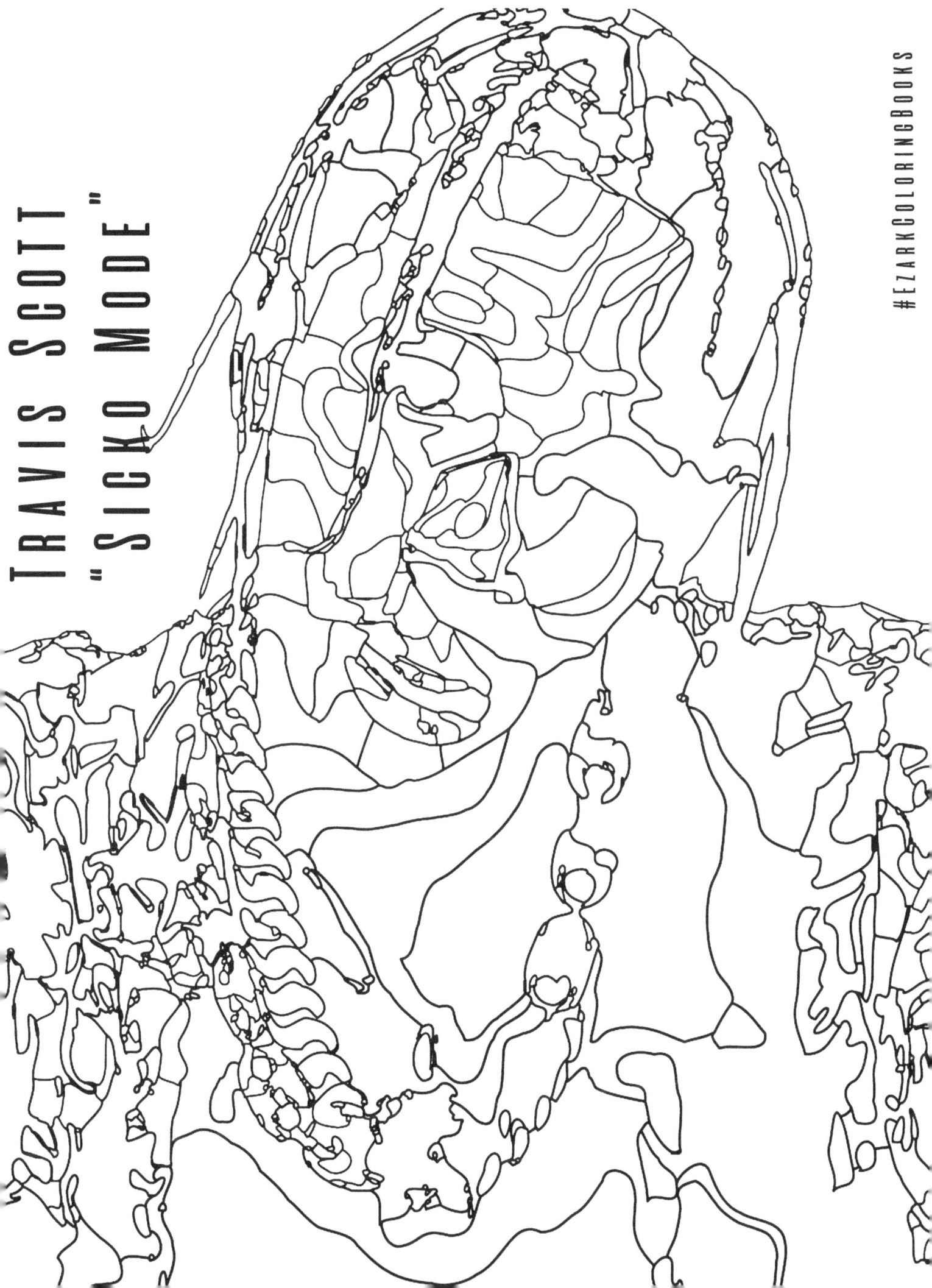

TRAVIS SCOTT "SICKO MODE"

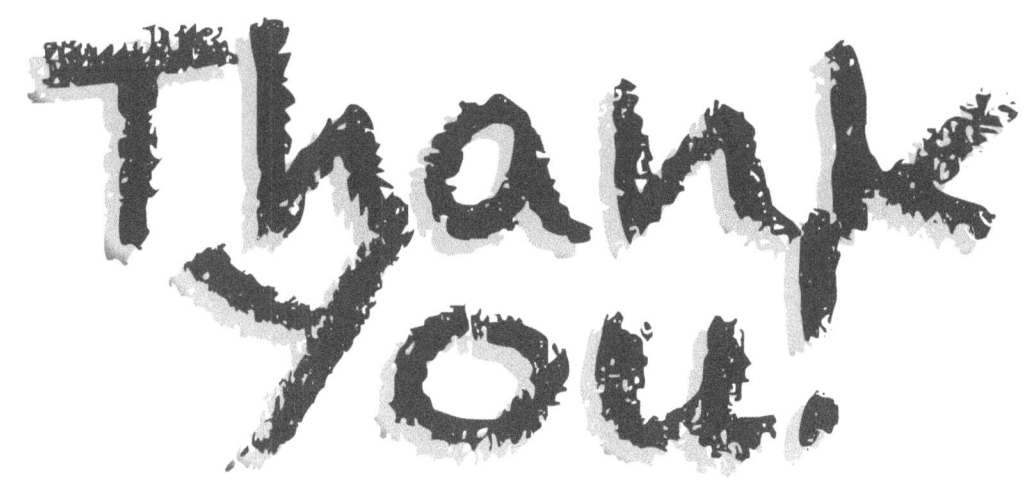

I'D LOVE YOUR FEEDBACK. PLEASE SEND

ME AN EMAIL WITH ANY COMMENTS/QUESTIONS

YOU MAY HAVE: EzarkNYC@gmail.com

Stay tuned for October's issue!

Availible for pre-order September15th

www.EzarkNYC.com